AF471748

Poems and Stories from a Prisoner's Troubled Heart

By

Peter Knoester

AuthorHouse™
1663 Liberty Drive
Bloomington, IN 47403
www.authorhouse.com
Phone: 1-800-839-8640

First published by AuthorHouse 06/2/2011

ISBN: 978-1-4567-4311-6 (sc)

Library of Congress Control Number: 2011906084

Printed in the United States of America

This book is printed on acid-free paper.

Foreword

I wrote these stories and poetry about people who are or who were incarcerated at one time or another and did experience the heartaches and sorrows this brings. Needless to say that anyone reading this booklet does not have to be an ex-con or prisoner to understand what I am talking about. Having had to do with prisoners as well as with people who were incarcerated at one time and having heard their stories I decided to write about it and perhaps prevent others especially the teenagers of today of going through what they went through, losing house and home, family and friends because of what they did which made them outcasts of society. My writing may seem a bit amateurish and I am sure could do with some improvement but that is just me and I wrote what came to my heart and mind.

Words come to me at times at their own volition and I need to write them down as they come, before my mind turns to other things. I wrote a poem some time ago about poetry and it goes like this:

Talk of the heart is poetry
That untapped well that dwells in me
Where words by thousands do abide
They do come out deep in the night
They come to form a line or two
They come to speak to me and you

Table of Contents

Cry of the Heart

Betrayal it is so hard to take
More so when so much is at stake
A friendship lost won't come again
As it comes just now and then
It's absence causes heartfelt pain
That it leaves scars is very plain
A trusted friend is hard to find
I hope that you keep that in mind

My mind it wanders far away
Remembering another day
When things were good and also clear
Not like now so full of fear
Oh future what have you in mind
Will you be gentle, will you be kind?
To bite the bullet this I must
And in my God I put my trust

My prayer

Oh God, my maker to Thee I pray
Come to my help without delay
My sins they weigh me down so much
Thou seems so far and out of touch
Please reach out and take my hand
Let there between us be a band
Don't let me ever lose my way
Cause I don't want to go astray

I have a God, Who's name is light
Who puts all my foes to flight
Embrace me Father of all men
I will love Thee Thou knows I can
Enable me to see Thy love
One tiny second is enough
This will last my whole life through
Than I won't stray but will be true

Please hear my cry

Who will see her cry
Or who will hear her weep
Afraid she is the fist will fly
Now she's bereft of sleep

The one she loves, he is so mad
At everything she says
She doesn't know why he's like that
Her life it is a mess

She knows that something must be done
To stop the hurt and pain
But for the kids she long be gone
That she can't leave is plain

When looking in the glass
She sees her swollen face
Remembering the way it was
Before all this took place

Oh why is he the one
Who caused such untold grief
When seeing what that man has done
It is beyond belief

What man is he to act that way
A root cause must there be
Why don't this man get up and say
There's someone I must see

Too people that will gave him aid
With the rage that lives within
Who knows it may be not too late
For a new life to begin

The man in the glass

When you get what you want in a struggle for yourself
And the world makes you king for a day
Just go to the mirror and look at yourself
And see what that man has to say

For it isn't your father, mother or wife
Whose judgment upon you must pass
The fellow whose verdict counts most in you
Is the one staring back from the glass

Some people may think, you're a straight shooting chum
And call you a wonderful guy
But the man in the glass says you are only a bum
If you can't look him straight in the eye

He's the fellow to please, never mind all the rest
For he is with you clear to the end
And you have passed the most dangerous and difficult test
If the man in the glass is your friend

You can fool the whole world down the pathway of life
And get pats on the back as you pass
But your final reward will be heartaches and tears
If you cheat the man in the glass

From the AA people

Closing down the house of correction

The place is called house of corrections
Inside this place are many sections
Some have a name and some a number
That's where all the inmates slumber
They all stay here until their trial
Some stay short, some quite a while
Within a year we all be gone
And than you see there be no one
This place will than be closing down
And all the inmates will be gone

Officer of corrections

I am an officer of correction
And I want things done to near perfection
I don't take gaff from anyone
And I don't care what you have done
When I'm around you show respect
Cause if you don't you may get decked
Don't ever say you ain't been told
Just in case you're being bold
The common thing between me and you
Is just like you, I am in jail too

Love

The path of love is full of thorns
Of roses that have died
I saw the one, who now scorns
The man she loved, who lied

The roses that were beautiful
Have long withered away
Attraction has now lost it's pull
And words have lost their sway

Is it true that one can un-love
The person once held dear?
We pray to heaven high above
As answers are unclear

What happened in the distant past
Has now come to the fore
How long now will this burden last
Will it be for evermore?

They say, "You should start anew"
As everything is lost
As you can see I'm very blue
When thinking of the past

The past is where I live today
Where else is there to go?
Those memories, they have a way
To make me love it so

The one I loved, she still is there
Waiting for me to come
There, is no burden that I bear
It's there, that I have freedom

My child

Oh child of mine I hurt you so
The sorrows fill my heart
In ignorance I did not know
How much of this would smart

I think of you when I'm awake
And pray the Lord will bless
While hope I did not take away
Your pursuit of happiness

Because of past deeds done
I'm feeling mighty low
For you I may as well be gone
As now you hate me so

Please ask yourself this question now
If everything was bad
While thinking back with puckered brow
About the good times had

I beg of you don't look at me
With malice in your heart
When doing this it well can be
Forever we will part

Forgiveness may be just a word
That's sometimes used in vain
But please don't cut the slender cord
Because you have such pain

I want to see and hug you close
But you're so far away
It would be better for us both
And family to stay

As family it's all we got
Like me don't throw away
This precious link that seems too hot
Please don't let it decay

The one I love

My dear's brown hair is streaked with grey
She's getting old to my dismay
One thing is sure we can't hold time
So getting old, that is no crime
My love's green eyes, they still do shine
I thank the Lord that she is mine
Her heart, it is so understanding
Her love for me is never ending
The strength she has it comforts me
Without her love I can not be
She knows I love her very much
At night I'm longing for her touch
To grow old together would be fine
Please tell me, you're that girl of mine

A prisoner's plight

They heard the prosecutor tell
This man belongs into a cell
The days of freedom they are gone
The yearning for them have began
The count has started one, two, three
Until the day we will be free

Although we cried a thousand tears
The real mender will be years
Because time it heals every wound
Even though they say it wouldn't
We will prevail and love again
While thinking back now and then

The edge of crime that we fall off
Into the abyss which never has enough
Of people, it's mouth is wide agape
We should avoid it like the plague
However if we would go astray
The system then will have it's way

The guards are not there to tuck you in
For some it becomes a loony bin
The strong will cower those who're weak
With a future that's really bleak
The people we meet, they come and go
But in the end there's freedom, this I know

Past Joy

There was a joy that I have known
That's gone now, oh where has it flown
Come back to me, that is my wish
As I can't live without this

The proof of youth lies in their strength
That will remain to quite some length
Until the day when they grow old
And then they won't be quite so bold

I am a grownup now a man
I always do the best I can
Sometimes however I will stray
And then it seems I lost my way

I am a man who has a wife
In her I have a mate for life
She's made of spice and oh so sweet
She's the nicest person that you meet

I am a wrong that can't be righted
At least to those who are short sighted
Correct the wrong, by good deeds done
Before you know, the wrong is gone

I am the truth and reign supreme
To some though, I am just a dream
That turn the truth into a lie
It often makes me wonder why?

I am the law and I am firm
When breaking me, I make you squirm
The judge can sentence you to jail
And then you cry to no avail

There is a road that's very wide
On which a lot of people stride
The end of which does lead to hell
Please do remember this real well

There is a road that's really narrow
That is the one that you should follow
The end of which is heaven bound
Make sure on this road you are found

Our guilt

Our guilt is drowned in pools of tears
The wrong we did to all those dears
We rue the day when we were born
When others look at us with scorn

The wrongs we did we can not right
Not with the tears we cry at night
Let us not fall in hopelessness
As this will add to our distress

The judge will tell you, what is what
When all involved, will have a chat
Our jail term may be not really fair
But to protest, we do not dare

The time we spent behind the bars
Will surely leave a lot of scars
When in the end freedom is won
A careful life style has began

We can not shed the stigma of jail
The more we try the more we fail
Though on the surface we seem to be
But are we ever truly free?

Oh cruellest of heart whom has thou slain
Whom in the cold, cold ground is lain
Doest thou not care to whom thou impart
The terrible things born in thy heart

Why were thou born why must thou be
Why pray to God on bended knee
Why hypocrite should He forgive
Why should He change the life you live

Thou art the one beyond a doubt
From thee these evil thoughts went out
To blame the others is not fair
So see to it that thou don't dare

And now the love bonds they are broke
The one's who cared threw off that yoke
They shut thee out that's what they've done
For them thou may as well be gone

Now if thou cried a thousand tears
And rued thy deeds for years and years
Thou can't undo things done by thee
Yes I am the one yes even me

What is truth

The truth is sometimes idly used
And sometimes it gets real abused
Half truths are sometimes worse than lies
Sometimes they stay until one dies
Then in the cold, cold grave they go
And then no one will ever know

The victims words are always true
But not the criminal's, which is you
Your words when spoken must be lies
It does not matter if one cries
Your sobs and tears on deaf ears fall
You are the worse one of them all

The locks go click in early morn
Just when a brand new day is born
Then we get up and make our bed
And then our breakfast we will get
Some times it's eggs or it is beans
You're kept alive by any means

Within the jail

When looking out at dawn of day
I see the buildings drab and grey
The cells is where the people sleep
It's there where some of them do weep
Remorse and sorrow, for those who will
For others there is hatred still

Who is the one who'll set us free
From our minds wiles and tyranny
This freedom may be easily gained
By one who knows and it's explained
Then sadness turns to happiness
The one who does this God will bless

My youth

Oh youth of mine where have you flown
Not long ago, you were my own
Now that we have gone our separate ways
Though far away I see your distant rays
Now I'm getting old and grey
You could say, I've seen my day
The embers smoulder deep within
But they are getting oh so dim
I hope to grow old gracefully
It would make a better me

Is it possible?

Is it possible to fall out of love
Is all what passed in vain
Why was the bond not strong enough
Why am I in such pain

What Happened to that tenderness
Why must I feel so low
Must I embrace this loneliness
Why didn't our love grow

So speedily the time went by
My life it was secure
Now all I had, it went awry
Of life I am not sure

I flee into myself for thought
But answers I don't get
My guess is, it was all for naught
So were the tears I shed

Oh Lord have pity on my soul
Don't let me pine away
To be with Thee that is my goal
No matter what they say

A promise given and not kept
Is just an idle thing
A boundary was overstepped
A deed that sorrows bring

As I look back in time a while
And see the road behind
My face breaks out into a smile
The time then, it was kind

To see the ruins by and by
It breaks my heart you know
It all gives me more tears to cry
What can I do, I loved her so

Pre-trial

His life right now it is in limbo
What will happen, he don't know
It's like a dream and not reality
His mind's eye tries but can not see
The end of the road that he is on
He feels just like that long lost son
Who yearned to see his family
But he must wait until he's free
It could be that even then
They won't take him back again
The sorrow caused and all the pain
May be all that will remain
And then the loneliness sets in
When he's deprived of all his kin
To start anew he does not dare
Besides he does not really care
His life comes slowly to an end
And death is just around the bend
His soul will leave his body then
To be with the ones he loved, again

The rain

The rain outside echoes the feelings of my heart
It is this emotion that surrounds me for a while now
My heart tries to fly back to the time I was happy
But my heart does not fly on broken wings
How wretched I am, don't you see that, how lonely
Why don't you all reach out and express your love?
Is there none now, are all too busy to see my plight?
I know forgiveness does not come easy for most people
And to withhold that most important part of living
Is that not the purpose in our lives, or is it?
Yes, when making your own bed, you must sleep in it
We all know that and to say it does not make things better
I want to lay down in the rain and get a cleansed soul
What a feeble attempt to get a clear conscience
Reality is ever there, but I can dream can't I?

The sting of hopelessness

Oh death me in thy arms do take
But please be kind for heaven sake
Don't hurt me more than I can stand
Just make of this my life an end
Why don't you come when I'm asleep
And let not anybody weep
Let no one come and see my grave
Not even those who's life I gave
No one will miss my being here
Not even those whom I held dear
So death please take me by the hand
And lead me then to a new land

A prayer from within

Dear Father to Thee I pour out my soul
To be with Thee that is my goal
My life, my mind it is so weary
From all this load that I do carry
Forgive my sins I did commit
I was like a mule without a bit
No bridle led to a road that's straight
It's for Thy mercy that I wait
In Thy forgiveness is my hope
The reason with this life I cope

Bereft

Bereft I am of family and friends
And now the grief it never ends
Only the memories remain
I hope from hatred they refrain
For love is the very thing I need
It covers all my sins indeed
A love alone it can not grow
And when it dies one feels so low

So long guys

Now that I've gone to another place
We will go our separate ways
You may think, who was that man
Think good of me for those who can
I am a man who went astray
But I am looking for the day
When all of us, yes you and me
Get out of jail and will be free

Getting old

The words I wrote look back at me.
I'll swear the dotted i's can see.
What do they see? A man old and grey.
A person who has seen his day,
But now is feebly hanging on,
Until his days on earth are done.

Talk of the heart

Talk of the heart is poetry.
That untapped well that dwells in me,
Where words by thousands do abide,
They do come out, deep in the night.
They come to form a line or two,
They come to speak, to me and you.

Seasons

The seasons they just come and go.
Like ocean tides they have their flow.
Like twilight comes before the night.
Like dawn that comes before it's light.

Why

Why have winter, summer, fall,
What is the purpose of it all?
It's the reason we feel alive,
The will to live, which is the drive.

To feel happiness and also sorrow.
And to look forward to tomorrow.
Without this hope, there's no desire,
We may get stuck, in this world's mire

Spring

In spring all birds they chirp away,
At early morn each brand new day.
To hear them sing elates my heart,
The year again has a new start.

Again all things wake up and grow.
It makes me happy, this I know.
As I am too, to this a part,
It's just like having a new start.

Thoughts in Flight

When thoughts are in flight and look down on the barren fields of nothingness
Wanting to reach out and bring life where there is just mental dust
How it aches and tries to influence that part which is dying for the lack of will.
Oh let there be a miracle which causes that which is dead to come alive
And breath in again that life force that seem to be forgotten and put away
Into that part of the mind where there are so many reminders of life within
Please utter the words which will be the evidence that not all is lost
And emerge from the dark side of the mind to again be the power of old.
To rejuvenate the mind and let the soul hear the music of the harp softly played
And be satisfied with that old saying, that hope is indeed Spring eternal.

Beyond Our Mind

Beyond the realm we call our mind,
There is a world that is not kind.
Some mountains look so harsh and cold,
And deserts that are dry I am told.
The poles are where the ice kings reign
And in their grip the poles remain

A Thought

What is that thought that nags at me,
I know it's there, but I can't see.
It may be good, it may be bad.
I hope it does not make me sad.

Besides there is no room for thought,
So that this one, comes to naught,
And then it will stop nagging me,
Then from that one, I'll be free.

Love

I looked at her and she at me.
Our love, I knew, could never be.
So part we did, it was so hard,
Because it was sure to break her heart.
Now I'm alone and feel so lost.
I am engulfed with memories past.

The meadow

As I am walking along my road on this early Sunday morning, I come to a misty meadow where half a dozen cows and their calves are grazing. They look at me with big opaque eyes that are like deep pools of black water. It does not take the calves long to get used to me staring at them, as they realize that I mean them no harm. Soon they are darting around on stiff legs to express the life force that is within them. I almost burst out in laughter to see them frolic like that, but I dare not as it would be like disturbing the peace. Some flies are flitting about and seek out the fresh cow dung. A bumble bee hums right around my head, startling me, as they have been known to sting people, I leave him alone. High aloft are a few wispy clouds heralding the coming of another beautiful day. I smell the dew on the grass, and the early morning light bounces and gleams off anything that is wet. The glare is hard on my eyes, but I love it so, as the world around me seems to be made of gold and silver. The night moths have settled down, and the butterflies are already busy pollinating the road side flowers and weeds. The morning mist is now rising as the sun gains its strength and evaporates the moisture from the plants and grasses, all too soon in my opinion, but we must all abide by the rules and laws of nature.

A sudden strong breeze whips through the quiet meadow, picks up the vapours and driving them into the trees surrounding the meadow. Everything is seen very clear now. All too soon, all too soon, my heart says, but I know that nothing lasts forever, as time moves on with unstoppable force and even this fine Sunday morning must come to an end.

The Mighty Oak

Oh mighty oak, thou hast been slain.
Thou hast succumbed to wind and rain.
A mighty wind, it howled and blew.
The power of which, thou never knew.

No birds again will nest in thee,
For now, thou art, a fallen tree.
Thy branches were high in the sky,
But now on muddy ground they lie.

Thy leaves will soon wither away,
They will not see another day.
Thou shall be missed, by all who see,
But most by me, as I loved thee.

www.ingramcontent.com/pod-product-compliance
Ingram Content Group UK Ltd.
Pitfield, Milton Keynes, MK11 3LW, UK
UKHW041833200726
13854UKWH00003BA/1115